D1383898

COUNTRY LIVING

The New Look of Country

Text by Rhoda Murphy

Foreword by Nancy Mernit Soriano

HEARST BOOKS

A Division of Sterling Publishing Co., Inc.

NEW YORK

Copyright © 1999 by Hearst
Communications, Inc.

This book was previously published as
a hardcover under the title *Country Living
Decorating Style: The New Look of Country*

All rights reserved.

Produced by Smallwood & Stewart, Inc.,
New York City
Editor: Maria Menechella
Designer: Susi Oberhelman

Library of Congress Cataloging-in-
Publication Data available upon request.

10 9 8 7 6 5 4 3 2 1

First Paperback Edition 2004
Published by Hearst Books
A Division of Sterling Publishing Co., Inc.
387 Park Avenue South, New York, NY 10016

Country Living is a trademark owned by
Hearst Magazines Property, Inc., in USA, and
Hearst Communications, Inc., in Canada.
Hearst Books is a trademark owned by Hearst
Communications, Inc.

www.countryliving.com

Distributed in Canada by Sterling Publishing
℅ Canadian Manda Group, One Atlantic
Avenue, Suite 105
Toronto, Ontario, Canada M6K 3E7

Distributed in Australia by Capricorn Link
(Australia) Pty. Ltd.
P.O. Box 704, Windsor, NSW 2756 Australia

Printed in China

1-58816-364-4

CONTENTS

ONE OF OUR FIRST BOOKS WAS CALLED *Country Living Country Decorating*, a comprehensive look at country style in America. It was an ambitious undertaking, one that we felt would stand the test of time. But the meaning—and the look—of country has continued to evolve in the years since we first published *Country Decorating* (and in the 25 years since the launch of *Country Living* magazine). As a decorating style it has become even more encompassing, mixing old with new, formal with informal, and period styles with flea market finds. It continues to honor the past—but with a new vitality and spirit that makes *The New Look of Country* the perfect complement to today's lifestyle. It is a look that can be simple and sophisticated, rustic and retro, but also comfortable and inviting—a look that is truly American.

FOREWORD

What follows on these pages is a celebration of country style today: of old buildings lovingly restored: new houses mindful of the past, and rooms that speak volumes about individual expression and the universal appeal of the country lifestyle. We've taken a new look at the Capes, saltboxes, cabins, and barns that we love, and explored the rooms that make them classic and so much a part of our national character.

We hope you will find inspiration here, as well as renewed enthusiasm for what we believe to be the best of American country today.

NANCY MERNIT SORIANO
Editor-in-Chief

A Hou

PART ONE

se in the COUNTRY

AMERICAN COUNTRY HAS MANY faces, shaped by different periods, places, and people. Our heritage encompasses such diverse elements as the elegant Federal-style row-houses of Eastern cities like Philadelphia and Boston, the log-dwellings of early Mid-western settlers, and the adobe structures of the Southwest. Regional architectural and decorating differences were—and to an extent still are—dictated by climate, light, and terrain. The brilliant desert weather of the Southwest, for instance, requires a different design approach than the more muted sunlight and changing seasons of New England. Some homeowners choose to follow the spirit of their house when decorating, others enjoy mixing regional themes. It is this decorating freedom that gives country its broad appeal and defines American country style—to put it simply, there's something in it for everyone. ■

American VERNACUL

The NORTHEAST

A boys-camp bunkhouse became a cute summer cottage thanks to a husband and wife who overhauled it and filled it with painted furniture and cheerful textiles. Foul-weather gear is always ready by the front door in a lift-top bench (opposite). A grain-painted navigational box from the early 1800s rests on top. A trip to Sweden inspired the owners to paint the doors yellow and the floors white, and to place a green cupboard in the living room (above left). Open shelving and painted beadboard cabinets with playful fish pulls lend charm to the tiny kitchen (above right).

DESIGN IN THE NORTHEAST is shaped by the history of the area. The homes here range from a rustic cottage on Maine's rocky coast, to an elegant brownstone in New York City, to an old farmhouse in the hills of Pennsylvania. Although the settings differ, the mission of the homeowners is the same—to fill their homes with objects they love. As one homeowner puts it: "We didn't have a big decorating budget, but that was all right because we just wanted the place to make us smile."

A sophisticated country style looks quite at home in a one-bedroom apartment in Brooklyn. The owner started with a few dramatic pieces of dark cherry furniture, then added color and pattern. The dining room pedestal table is one of those cherry pieces (above). Checks on one set of chairs and solids on another keep the pattern from looking too busy. The dining area's hanging rack was custom-built from fiberboard, an engineered-wood product. Even a small room can handle an oversized piece of furniture. In the living room (right), a massive armoire anchors the space and serves as a much-needed focal point. The dining room chairs can easily be moved in here when extra seating is needed.

A steady style and similar colors are a must in a small space, especially an apartment. To give their 1949 apartment in New York City a fresh look, a couple turned to yellow walls and textured fabrics. Complementary colors and patterns pull the living area together (top left). Linen curtains edged with gold echo the sofa's tones and the pale lemon of the walls. Lampshades that resemble pouffy hats pick up the chairs' striped motif. The owners highlighted the green wallpaper in the bedroom (bottom left) with green accents such as the chair in the corner (a flea-market find), the glass lamp by the bed, and a collection of art pottery.

A quilt expert turned her Manhattan flat into a calm backdrop for her handiwork. A wool Victorian variation quilt claims attention in the living room (opposite top left). On the other side of the room, a circa 1910 white-on-red Flying Geese variation hangs. Several antiques from the owner's home state of Kentucky—including the late 1800s hanging cupboard—populate the entry hall (opposite top right). Large baskets beneath a farm table (opposite bottom) provide storage space for the owner's quilts and allow her to change her wall art at will.

Tucked away in the rolling meadows of eastern Pennsylvania, a 1700s fieldstone farmhouse was transformed into the Auldridge Mead Inn. Period pieces and old paint treatments bring 18th-century flavor to the historic house. A pair of Shaker-made children's chairs from the late 1800s and a set of old ice skates appear as sculpture when hung from a peg rail in one of the guest rooms (above). A small-scale horse-and-heart stencil rings the room. Craftsman Craig Mattoli (who owns the inn along with master chef Karyn Coigne) sponge-painted the mantel and doorway of a guest room (right) then coated them with a dark-red oil glaze. At the foot of the 19th-century mahogany spool bed sits an impressive Sheraton-style Maryland blanket chest dating to the early 1800s.

The MIDWEST

Artwork takes on three dimensions in an Illinois collector's renovated farmhouse. In the living room (opposite), each piece was carefully chosen for its texture and patina, including an arrow weathervane and a salvaged fanlight transom. A guest room (above left), christened the green room for its verdant touches, features an architectural fragment with cutout stars hanging above a mid-19th-century rope bed. Pillows made from worn-out wool blankets support an Amish doll in another guest room (above right). A salvaged "eyebrow" screen accents the wall.

STRADDLED BY THE two coasts, the Midwest takes its cues from both. From the East there is a love of fine-lined pieces and patterns and Victoriana (the period when much of the Midwest was settled), while from the West comes a preference for rugged pioneer pieces and a pristine backdrop of whites. These homes run the architectural gamut, from an updated Illinois farmhouse, to a new home in a suburban housing development, to an ornate Italianate mansion in Ohio. The owners—all inveterate collectors—rely on intriguing objects to bring character to their homes.

An Italianate Victorian mansion in Ohio with eleven-foot ceilings and eight-foot windows provides a grand setting for a varied collection of objects. During the remodeling of the kitchen, the owners had to remove two false ceilings to find the original (top left). The cabinetry was made using salvaged materials. A metal restaurant cart acts as a moveable island. A collection of antique toys that the husband had in childhood decorates a shelf in their baby's room (left). A giant shoe—a tradesman's sign from the early 20th century—sits atop a dining room cupboard (top right). Voile curtains separate the dining room and parlor (opposite). The columns were salvaged from another old mansion. Cotton duck sleeves cover the 1890s chairs. The chandelier is a wrought-iron auction find—the couple added the crystal beads.

A suburban community center in Illinois proves that development houses need not be featureless. Broad rattan wing chairs and a cotton rug lend gracious informality to the living room (left). The look and colors of vintage textiles are recalled in both rug and fabrics. Slim-lined and armless, the dining chairs (top right) offer comfort in a tight space and invite lingering. In both the living and dining rooms, wood blinds cover the large windows, allowing for abundant light and privacy while drawing attention to the furnishings. Quiet neutral colors make the bedroom a restful spot (bottom right). The upholstered footboard and headboard echo the dining room chairs; sheer roman shades on the windows filter light beautifully.

The S O U T H

Two deteriorating pre–Civil War log cabins were reincarnated as this 10-room log home in central Mississippi. History means much to the couple who owns the cabin—they dine with the same pewter cutlery (with deer-antler handles) that the wife's family has used for three generations. They set their early 1800s dining table with mid-19th-century yellow-ware, and decorate the antique pine shelf in their kitchen with pantry boxes (opposite). A mid-1800s table and plank-bottom chairs furnish the sunporch (above). An occasional alligator can be seen lurking about the 2,500-acre property.

THE SOUTH HAS ALWAYS been a complicated place, and its homes illustrate just how heterogeneous—and deeply fascinating—it remains. A Mississippi log house, constructed from pre–Civil War dwellings; a newly linked pair of 19th-century cabins in Kentucky; a Federal period row house in Old Town Alexandria, Virginia; and a historic Florida cottage made from cypress and coral—are all revitalized with modern touches and yet still pay tribute to their Southern past.

here used to be two main buildings on Cabin Creek Farm in Kentucky: Hannah and Art Stearns's shop (a 100-year-old building) and their home, an 1863 poplar log cabin 50 feet away. Tired of shuttling back and forth, they designed a link between the two cabins. The couple collected aged doors, antique timbers, and old white furniture to make the new section appear as aged as the two structures it joins. Cabin Creek is famous for its signboards; two of their best-sellers hang in the kitchen (above). To create an old-barn feeling, Art installed old rugged beams. White-washed walls and a yellow floor transformed the keeping room (right). One beam had never been stained and was left untouched for posterity.

"I am a purist when it comes to restoration," states the owner of a 1795 row house in Alexandria, Virginia. He has filled his restoration project with fine regional antiques of the period. A carved tester bed from Virginia replete with its original hardware stars in the bedroom (top left). The mahogany armoire (above) by Alexandria furniture maker William Muir dates to about 1825. A free-standing tub, dated 1922, dominates the bathroom (bottom left), which is outfitted with a 19th-century fancy chair. In the second-floor parlor (opposite), the plastering remains unpainted. A rare circa 1825 marble-top center table stands beneath a French lighting fixture of the same period. Blue fabric turns a circa 1820 Baltimore sofa into an eye-catcher.

Character abounds in a 1930s coral-rock cottage in Coral Gables, Florida. Ever thrifty, the man who built the Depression-era house formed the cottage's walls with coral rock left over from the 1923 construction of a public pool. Inspired by the tilework, the current owners chose red and green paint for the walls, trim, and beams throughout the house. In one of the house's bathrooms (above), original hand-painted tiles depict the colorful escapades of Don Quixote. To create the spacious living room (right), the architect/owner enclosed the original central courtyard .

THE AMERICAN WEST has always been a land of extremes—and not just geographically. It has long been a place where people could reinvent themselves and test every boundary. There is free-wheeling California, unbounded by convention, and always on the cutting edge. There is rugged Colorado with its dry deserts and craggy mountains. And there are all the places in between, where individual expression is both admired and expected.

The Western houses featured here truly epitomize their surroundings. A Los Angeles home boasts brilliant colors on walls and countertops

The WEST

A Los Angeles couple revamped the galley kitchen (opposite) of their 1930s home simply by playing up the room's vintage charms, punctuating the cabinetry with Bakelite pulls and adorned hand-painted shelves with 20th-century kitchenware (above). But the room's piece-de-resistance is the floor made by a local artist. She took pieces of vinyl-composition tile—the heavy-duty material on many supermarket floors—in a multitude of colors to create an unforgettable and highly durable mosaic.

and a floor worthy of a modernist painter. Configured from late 18th-century rural buildings, another California home could not be more different, but is perfectly suited for its mountainous setting in the Santa Ynez Valley. Colorado is represented by an extraordinary century-old ranch house with a 1940s extension that combines classic Western elements—log furnishings, for instance, with unexpected softening touches like brass beds covered with floral comforters.

Much of America is represented in this country home in Santa Ynez, California, 150 miles north of Los Angeles. The structure combines a hay barn from New Hampshire with two West Virginia log homes and a Tennessee log cabin—all of late 18th-century vintage. Painted Windsors encircle a late 18th-century painted Pennsylvania hutch table (top left). Perched on a Shaker blanket chest, a sculptural weathercock adorns one corner of the living room (above). The exposed logs of one of the cabins serve as artwork in the master bedroom (bottom left), where a grain-painted blanket chest is paired with a sofa from the 1800s. The massive fireplace in the great room (opposite) was modeled after early New England hearths and was pieced together from serpentine, a local rock.

A half-mile stretch of the South Platte river helped shape this late-1800s Colorado ranch house. The house was built with stones culled from the river bed and with local lumber. The diamond-paned window in a guest room (above) is one of several Tudor-style accents in the house. Vintage iron bedsteads and an old chair painted green furnish country comfort. The dining room (left) showcases an Adirondack-style table and hutch and a leaded-glass chandelier. The ceiling's stenciled and freehand designs evoke Native American motifs. A 1940s addition, the enclosed porch overlooks the river (opposite). New hickory furnishings complement the log walls and ceiling, and an antique sepia print sits above the fireplace.

The SOUTHWEST

A cedar-log home is one of five 19th-century houses for guests of the Settlement House. In the living room (opposite), a mid-1800s sofa covered in cowhide pairs with a twig side table and an early 19th-century pine armoire. Antlers shed by deer support the valances. In the Cowboy room (above left), one of three guest rooms, a 1940s child's saddle matches the linens on the iron bed. Benches salvaged from a Texas church provide seating for a long pine dining table (above right). On the table an early 1800s Apache water jug made of pine bark, needles, and sap makes a sturdy vase.

SOME HOUSES OF THE Southwest represent the past of this region, others its present. The Settlement House at Round Top, in Texas, is an inn made up of four historic buildings. Legend has it that Confederate soldiers encamped on the land and helped the German settlers who owned the property erect the frame. "It's a sin to let an old place that has potential go," says owner Karen Beevers. Beevers's sentiments are shared by painter and antiques dealer Jean Jack, whose new adobe-style house in Santa Fe, New Mexico, is layered with intriguing folk art from around the country.

Artist Jean Jack has adorned her adobe-style home in Santa Fe with her own paintings and an extensive collection of folk art. Her wide-ranging eye can be seen in the living room (opposite), where a 1930s replica of a Davenport, Iowa, school rests on a coffee table made from a blacksmith's bellows. Colorful sap buckets from New England top a primitive late-1700s cupboard found in Indiana (above). A circa1860 weather-cock from Lancaster Country, Pennsylvania, presides over the antique dining table (top right) Jean bought from a Masonic lodge in Maine, then grain painted. Part of her yellowware collection sits in an 1869 Pennsylvania Dutch cupboard. Jean's grandchildren love the circa 1890 Mennonite trundle bed (bottom right) in the room.

Decorating with OLD GLORY

On June 14, 1777, the fledgling United States Congress adopted this resolution: "Resolved, that the Flag of the united states (sic) be 13 stripes alternated red and white, and the Union be 13 stars white in a blue field representing a new constellation." No one knows for certain who actually designed the flag; the Betsy Ross story has been dismissed by scholars as a myth. Whatever its origins, the flag has proved enduring, and its colors and patterns have become a classic—and foolproof—design accent.

Think of cheery red and white gingham, or blue-and-white striped ticking with red pillows for flair. The elements of the flag are also captivating—white stars, blue background, red stripes. Who can resist? The owner of a 1920s Southern California bungalow used flag accents to add flavor to her living room (below). Flying the flag is particularly a summer tradition, as it is outside an 1885 Long Island, New York, vacation home, or inside—draped over another American icon, a Windsor bench.

LIVING IN AN OLD HOUSE INVOLVES a lot of making do, of accepting certain quirks and idiosyncrasies as part of the package. New houses that borrow the best from historical homes are an ideal solution for anyone who wants to live with the past—but not live in it. A newly built structure can provide much of the delight of an old house with none of the drawbacks—or upkeep. Architects take the most appealing elements of traditional design—a gracious veranda, steeply pitched gables, or rough-hewn beams, for instance—and combine them with such contemporary features as a wide-open floor plan or an entire wall of view-revealing French doors. The homes in this chapter were inspired by three common historical styles: Carpenter Gothic, Cape Cod, and Saltbox. Despite their roots in the past, they are thoroughly modern living spaces. ■

New Homes CLASSIC ST

YLE

Carpenter GOTHIC

The gabled roof harks back to the home's Gothic Revival roots, yet the steep eaves and square porch columns represent modern flair (above). A pair of handsome stone chimneys are actually crafted from a manufactured stone material. The view from the front door spans the length of the house (opposite). Finely detailed octagonal columns define living areas (note the characteristic points on the columns) while keeping the space open. Throughout the first floor, practical and inexpensive laminate flooring keeps the backdrop light in feeling, while nine-foot ceilings lend graciousness.

IN THE 1830S, the Gothic Revival architectural style swept England. By the mid-19th century, it had migrated to these shores, influencing the look of many churches and colleges (Princeton University and the University of Pennsylvania, among them). For residences, America's abundance of timber and the invention of the jigsaw led to the creation of a more affordable wood version of Gothic style called Carpenter Gothic. A newly built cottage, on Washington State's Bainbridge Island, typifies the picturesque style, with its characteristic steeply pitched gables, broad veranda, and slightly pointed arches in the interior.

Though only 2,450 square feet, the cottage lives larger, thanks to an open floor plan, a combination kitchen/family room, and good acoustical separation between bedrooms. Modern materials, such as laminate flooring, fiberglass asphalt roof shingles, energy-efficient windows, and manufactured stone, made building it practical and also aided in stretching the tight budget.

Buttery yellow walls brighten the dining room and connect it visually to the front hall (above). Architectural heft comes from beadboard carried six feet up the walls. A limited decorating budget meant few extraneous fabric touches. A matchstick shade blocks direct light, while simple polyester voile panels add softness. The family room adjoins the kitchen, making one large living space (opposite). Pale apricot walls link the family room to the dining room. A mix of casual fabrics and informal upholstered pieces make it a room worthy of its name. With the appearance and texture of real rock, the rustic fireplace is actually made from manufactured stone, a blend of Portland cement, natural aggregates, and iron oxides.

A well-worn farm table replaces the expected island in the wide-open kitchen (opposite top). Vintage benches provide maximum seating. To reiterate the Gothic theme, a pointed arch frames the range, hood, and wall cabinets. The cabinetry deliberately evokes built-in Victorian dressers, rather than modern kitchen cabinets. In the master bath (opposite bottom), console sinks in periwinkle, a luxurious whirlpool bath, gleaming tile, and a tumbled marble floor inlaid with squares of purple glass make a mix of nostalgic ideas, modern technology, and welcome color. A contemporary air blends with the traditional in the master bedroom (right). A Biedermeier-style bed is topped by a stream-lined iron tester. White cotton bed hangings, loosely tied to the rods, evoke old-fashioned bed-dressings. Matching draperies and rods cover the oversized windows, which keep the bedroom flooded with light.

Period DETAILS

Like fossils in a rock, architectural details reveal much about the period of a house, even a newly built one. Two of the great hallmarks of the Carpenter Gothic style are decorative millwork and carved architectural elements. During the 1800s, these touches were made possible on a large scale by the newly invented jigsaw and allowed for an ornamentation that previously would have been too expensive for the middle classes. The Bainbridge Island house is rich in these elements.

Steep gables (top left), their shape accentuated by an inside arch, give the house its true character. Vertically layered plywood siding emphasizes the pitch of the gables. The multipaned, true-divided-light windows combine high energy efficiency with authentic period appearance. Custom-designed garage doors (bottom left) deliberately recall 19th-century carriage house entries. The arbor over the garage doors is ready to support climbing vines such as wisteria or grapes. Perhaps the most typical Carpenter Gothic element is the custom-designed newel post and banister (opposite). In an open floor plan, such decorative touches are necessary to make the stairs aesthetically pleasing.

A Cape Cod HOUSE

In the front hall (opposite), the bare essentials have taken on a kind of beauty. The floors are gleaming oak and the exposed staircase has been stripped to its bare-bones: treads, risers, and rail. The ceiling boasts beams that were rescued from an old house. Constructed from timber frames that were salvaged from four separate structures, the shingle-and-clapboard dwelling (above) is loosely based on rambling New England farmhouses of the 18th century. The telescoping design makes the 2,500-square-foot structure look bigger than it is.

EVER SINCE THE 17TH century, when the Pilgrims first created it, the sturdy house known as the Cape Cod has endured. Historical sources credit Yale president Timothy Dwight for coining the name in 1800. On a visit to Cape Cod, Dwight noted that nearly all the homes were similar: one-and-a-half stories high, with central chimneys, small windows, and gabled roofs. He called them "Cape Cod houses," and the name stuck.

The compactness and plainness of the Cape Cod design reflected a puritanical abhorrence for showiness of any kind. One Bostonian wrote, "There is…a remarkable republican simplicity in the style of buildings; little distinction that betokens wealth, an equality that extends to everything."

A new house in the Connecticut River Valley continues in that spirit. Built around an early 20th-century post-and-beam frame, the house shuns superficial ornamentation both inside and out. The facade features six-over-six paned windows, while the rear takes advantage of the river views with banks of sliding glass doors and windows. Despite the lack of frills, the house is infused with character, thanks to the many salvaged pieces used to build it.

G eorgia pine timbers salvaged from a circa 1910 silk mill in Lancaster, Pennsylvania, were recycled to construct the dwelling's stunning exposed framing. These powerful beams dominate the living room. A brick fireplace surround separates the living room from the entrance hall. Hand formed in wooden molds and kiln fired, the oversize Colonial-style bricks used to construct the wall were custom made in North Carolina.

A new soapstone wood-burning stove is as beautiful as it is functional in the family room (top left), which is open to both kitchen and dining room. Clock-maker Edward H. Stone of Maryland made the curly maple "coffin" wall clock, a reproduction of an 1810 timepiece. Inspired by Shaker case pieces, the kitchen's two-tone painted birch cabinetry includes freestanding china cupboards (bottom left). The early-20th-century ribbed glass lamps above the island were salvaged from a commercial building. A sliding glass center panel, engineered much like a pocket door, is all that separates the dining/family room from the outdoors (opposite). Windsor side chairs and a painted bench provide informal seating around the expandable cherry dining table.

A Salt BOX

WHEN THIS RHODE ISLAND couple set about to build an "Early American"-style house, they turned to the classic Saltbox, so called because the shape of the house resembled a Medieval saltbox. In the 1600s, few houses were built as Saltboxes. The lean-to in the back, which created the distinctive shape, was usually an addition.

For the wife, this home was a dream long in the making. She had been collecting pages from *Country Living* for years and knew exactly what she wanted. When she and her husband were ready to flesh out the bare interior of their newly constructed home, she went through the house nailing pictures to the exposed two-by-fours, illustrating the look she wanted in each room. Her husband, an electrical contractor by trade and a cabinetmaker by avocation, crafted many of the home's interior details, including molding, cabinetry, mantels, and even furniture. Over the years, they have completed the look with collections of antique pottery, textiles, and furnishings.

As befits the Colonial period which inspired it, the house is gracefully simple (above). No shutters detract from the paned windows, and a large central chimney anchors the house. The owner's cabinetry-making skills can be seen in the dining room's pine corner cupboard (opposite). He stained it to match the reproduction tavern table and Windsor chairs. In striving for a Colonial air, the owners left the beams exposed, painted the woodwork the muted green that would, in an old house, have come over time, and treated the windows to plain muslin tab curtains.

o be truly authentic, the house had to have a keeping room (opposite). Here, the owners dry herbs from their garden on the exposed oak beams. Stones salvaged from an 18th-century house lend the hearth a genuine period look. The homeowner crafted both the harvest table and the slant-back cupboard, which now houses a collection of turn-of-the-century yellowware. An early American homespun and a mid-19th-century coverlet dress the late-19th-century rope beds in a small bedroom (above) on the third floor of the house. The circa 1880 desk to the left of the window was made in upstate New York. The trunk at the foot of the low-post bed was a boyhood possession of the father of one of the owners.

IN THE 1890 SHORT STORY

The Revolt of Mother, Mary Wilkins Freeman tells a tale of a woman who gets so angry at her farmer-husband for spending all of their money on a new barn that she takes up residence there. At the time, the idea of living in a barn was unthinkable. But today, our sense of what makes a home has changed, and our desire to preserve any piece of the past we can seems to know no bounds. Rather than lose barns, garages, carriage houses, or former factories to the wrecking ball, people are rescuing them and reincarnating them as dwellings.

Old houses in particular are benefiting from renewed attention. Some homeowners undertake historically authentic restorations, filling their spaces with period pieces; others favor a more creative approach, combining original architecture with the modern embellishments they love. ■

Design RECONSID

ERED

Home CONVERSIONS

To evoke an ethereal mood in her New York City loft, the owner filled it with flea market finds and filmy fabric. She rescued the gothic arch in the living room (opposite) from a church in her Ohio hometown. A Victorian drapery panel dresses the daybed. A Hoosier cabinet top and Ohio relics such as a gym light fixture and a factory window outfit the kitchen (above left). Downtown breezes blow through the bathroom, where a faux-tile paint treatment covers up the once carpeted floor (above right).

THERE ARE TWO WAYS of treating a home that once was something else. The first is to disguise the past and create something altogether new. The second is to retain references to a home's earlier incarnation and even celebrate them. The woman who renovated a New York City loft followed the first approach, while two separate owners of barns took the second. All have succeeded in creating unique homes.

Several years ago, a Manhattan loft-dweller stared at her black plastered walls and industrial carpeting and decided it was time for a change. She exposed the apartment's original brick walls and wood flooring, then coated the walls in milky white paint and gathered lengths of diaphanous linen for the windows and for curtains between rooms.

The goal of the owner of a Long Island barn was to maintain the integrity of the structure's late 18th-century frame. To do so, he housed bedrooms and bathrooms in new additions so that the original building could serve as an undivided great room, incorporating the living, dining, and cooking areas.

Creating a sense of discrete spaces can be tricky in a loft. The owner divided up her square-footage with partial walls, filmy linen draperies, and furnishings—such as a decoupage screen, which separates the eating and cooking areas. For continuity she painted a harlequin-patterned floor, uniting the rooms in the commodious loft.

The glass-topped table was part of a vintage outdoor-furniture set. White vinyl chairs from the 1960s serve as comfy and informal dining chairs. Virtually all the furnishings in the home are salvaged pieces, most with their original paint. The owner's motto is simple: The more peeling paint, the better. It shows that a piece has lived.

To expose the barn's hand-hewn oak skeleton, he installed new white pine interior siding around it.

The owners of another barn on Long Island share the first owner's philosophy. They let the 19th-century barn itself dictate the direction of the project. The layout remains relatively unchanged from the original design, with a loft at either end and a central breezeway with rows of glass doors and windows replacing the traditional barn doors. Many of the unpretentious objects that decorate the barn, including farm tools and a dilapidated horse-drawn carriage, would be equally at home on a real farm. The owners even enclosed one of the lofts with netting so that the swallows could remain.

"Barns tend to be dark, so our design needed to bring in as much sunlight as possible," says the man who lives in a light-filled 200-year-old New Jersey barn, which he moved to Long Island, New York. Three pine boards from a late-19th-century barn were transformed into a massive 15-foot dining table (opposite). Remnants from a late-19th-century wrought-iron fence form the base. New red cedar shingles sheathe the original structure (top right), situated on one and a half acres. Across the kitchen ceiling, beams indicate the original divisions between the barn's stalls (right).

Guests of all ages love the bunk room in one of the barn's new additions (above). The owner installed authentic vintage radiators that he had sandblasted and repainted because they triggered fond memories of his childhood home. A freestanding fireplace functions as the focal point of the main living area and helps delineate dining and living rooms (right). The fireplace was placed here so that it would not obstruct the barn frame. Mismatched furnishings gathered during trips to flea markets give the interior a relaxed and accommodating atmosphere. "I chose materials that could take a beating," says the owner: old wood, wrought iron, stainless steel and canvas slipcovers.

When remodeling a circa 1869 barn, the two men who own it kept plenty of reminders of the structure's past life. Simple battens are part of those reminders, but new elements are also deliberately barn-like, such as the Dutch exterior doors (top left). The pair also layered their home with character-infused antiques such as the pie safe from the 1800s with pierced tin door fronts. The original hayloft forms the ceiling for one of the bedrooms (left). In the loft, the two store a carriage for their neighbor, whose family once owned the farmstead. The blue chest at the foot of the tester bed is a 19th-century reproduction of an Amish Bible box. Many of the pieces in the barn predate it. A pine cupboard (opposite) from Pennsylvania, made between 1820 and 1850, holds early-19th-century Staffordshire lusterware. The banister-back chair dates to the mid-1700s and wears at least four layers of paint.

Home RENOVATIONS

Fifty-five windows grace the century-old Queen Anne-style home (above); many of which look out onto Long Island Sound. A trompe l'oeil rug decorates the dining room's oak floor (opposite). The owner painted the flowers freehand, using blossoms from her garden as models. Four coats of polyurethane protect it. The ornately carved marble-topped buffet was in the house when the owners moved in; they believe it was made for the room.

TO RESTORE AN OLD structure—and make it livable—takes vision, patience, and often, a large budget. Perseverance is key; renovations can stretch out over decades. "In 36 years we have never stopped working on the place," laments the owner of an 18th-century Pennsylvania home. But what a restoration requires most of all is a passion for the character of the old house. It also takes the ability to see through old changes that detract from the home's original spirit, and the imagination to make

a relic from the past function for modern life. "Our house can be a slave driver," says the owner of a rambling Victorian, "but we love it nonetheless."

Each of the houses is different—a seaside Victorian replete with a turret and wide porches; an 1870 farmhouse made over in the Greek Revival style; an elegant Pennsylvania stone dwelling that was first built in 1740; and a 200-year-old Vermont farmhouse restored with attention both to historical accuracy and health concerns. They all have one thing in common: owners who look on the renovation of their homes as nothing less than an act of love.

T he original glazed fireplace tiles in the living room (opposite) dictated the room's color scheme. Against the tropical blue walls, a vintage quilt provides graphic drama. Elaborate woodwork adorns the house, particularly in the stairwell (top right). The detailing was first painted in the 1930s, and repeats the bead-and-panel pattern seen in all the rooms. Hidden in a third-floor room when the family bought the house in 1978, the twin iron beds (bottom right) weigh a ton, according to one of the owners. Instead of restoring the painted finish, she simply chipped away a little more paint to accentuate the patina (right).

The grand columns and porches notwithstanding, this home (above) was a plain-Jane 1870 farmhouse until an architect—a great fan of Greek Revival style—undertook its renovation. Going against the historical formula that called for important rooms to be at the front, the architect positioned the living room and master bedroom at the rear of the house, which gave them more privacy and better views. Rescued from a house that was demolished, an early-19th-century mantel serves as a model for the detailing on the coffered ceiling, built-in bookcases, and overmantel in the living room (right). The wide chestnut floorboards were discovered in the house's attic. A Hudson River School landscape hangs above the mantel.

he family that owns an old Pennsylvania farmhouse (the original structure dates from 1740, with additions in 1840, 1929, and 1991) has taken care to decorate it in a manner that befits its history, with fine Philadelphia-area antiques from the early 1800s. Brilliant yellow walls and 19th-century Canton porcelain distinguish the dining room (opposite), which is furnished with a circa 1815 table, a circa 1740 walnut Queen Anne highboy, and circa 1810 side chairs and armchairs made by Joseph B. Barry, a celebrated Philadelphia cabinetmaker. In the foreground, a copper urn rests atop a circa 1810 lyre-base worktable. Situated in the oldest section of the house, the living room (above) is formally appointed with 19th-century Philadelphia antiques, including a graceful circa 1810 sofa featuring carved feathers on its crest rail and a circa 1810 card table with brass accents. Both pieces have been attributed to Joseph B. Barry.

A Federal FARMHOUSE

AT FIRST, THE 1792 FARMHOUSE on 55 acres of land in Vermont seemed like a dream come true to the husband and wife who bought it. She had always hankered after an old house; he had long dreamed of having land. As time passed, however, the wife realized that she was getting sick fairly regularly and that her allergies were especially bothersome whenever she spent a lot of time in the house.

After hiring an environmental engineer, the couple discovered that the damp, inadequately insulated dwelling was plagued by 200 years worth of mold and mildew. To remedy the problem, the pair set out to make their house healthy as well as to restore it. In addition to disinfecting the entire structure and installing custom-made thermal windows with vintage glass, they brought wiring up to code and installed cotton insulation instead of the usual fiberglass. They also removed all lead-based paint and then finished walls, floors, and woodwork with all-natural paints, sealers, and stains.

L ocated on a quiet road in rural Vermont, the three-bedroom clapboard house (above) features a classic Federal-style center chimney and an entrance with transom and sidelights. During the renovation, the dining room's plaster ceiling was removed to expose its original beams (opposite). Save for a tasseled swag at the window, the room is virtually fabric-free so as to cut down on dust and other allergy-provoking substances. The almost stark decor suits the old farmhouse well; the absence of pattern makes the architecture and the lines of the country antiques stand out.

A newly-made, but period-appropriate mantel lends architectural presence to the parlor (above). It replaces a Victorian mantel. A large pattern covers the guest-room walls (left). It's the kind of paper that looks as though it's been there for 100 years, says the owner. Vintage cherry beds, a pine bureau, and a wire bench outfit the room. In the new garden room (right), pine ladder-backs surround a hutch table found in Vermont. Although the painted checkerboard floor isn't period-accurate, the owners love it anyway.

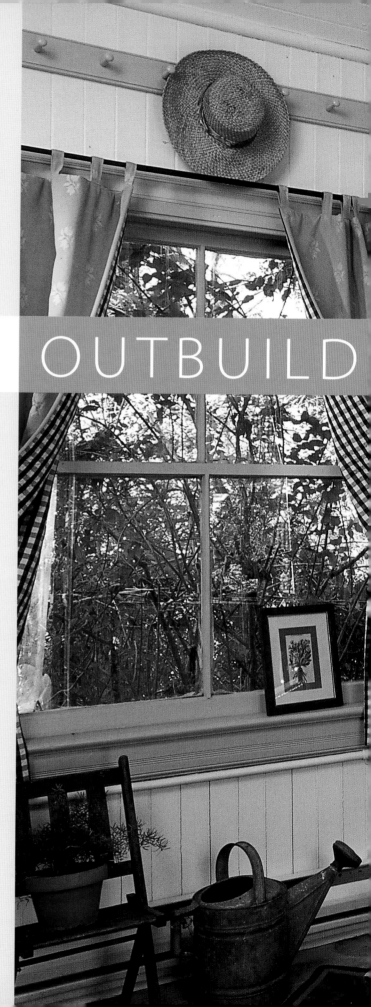

FOR A CHILD, AN OUTDOOR PLAY-
house is sheer heaven—a special, secret
place unbounded by rules, where imaginations can soar. Grown-ups as well take
delight in a tiny building where they have to
bend their heads to enter, where no one

New Spaces OUTBUILD

thinks to look for them and real life recedes.
Such a sanctuary can take many forms—it
can be a newly built guest cottage, a con-
servatory, or a writer's studio. Or it can be a
musty shed that has been cleaned up and
recast in a new role—as a gardener's getaway
perhaps, or a painter's atelier.

Such a spot offers an opportunity to
let the imagination soar. Homeowners can
exercise their creativity by painting it daring
shades, while decorating it with welcoming
furnishings and homey touches and filling it
with objects they love make it a true home
away from home. ■

Existing STRUCTURES

A storage shed, blessed with a high-pitched ceiling and fieldstone fireplace, became a welcoming gardener's retreat when the owners widened the front stoop and added window boxes and a stone path (above right). A closet now functions as the potting area (above left). Deep enough for filling watering cans, the original soapstone sink has generous work space (opposite). The shower is handy for cleaning up after a good day's work in the dirt.

IN THE SOUTH, outbuildings on a farm were known, quaintly enough, as dependencies. These extra buildings were dependent on the main house for necessities, but were separate entities, like children around a mother's skirt. Such additional buildings are fun to make over and even more fun to use. Often, they are very easily transformed—with a fresh coat of paint, a new floor, a clearing away of overgrown bushes, trees, and weeds—into spaces that are both intimate and inspiring.

n a previous life, a minute retreat (opposite) on an old Maryland farm was a washhouse.
Creative decorating brings the 12-by-12-foot space to life as a warm-weather hideaway.
Old scythes and baskets look like sculpture against whitewashed walls. A garland of dried lemon
leaves and lilies festoons the fireplace, a salvaged Federal-style pediment adorns the wall,
and buckets of freshly-cut blooms fill the air with scent. A homespun cotton dress makes a
decorative statement when hung on a wall (above left). Summer flowers gathered in
buckets create a seasonal mood in the cabin, where in good weather the door and
windows are always open. The old brick floor helps keep the space cool (above right).
Furnishings and walls were white-washed with watered-down latex paint for a crisp look.

New STRUCTURES

A **1920s picket fence from New England lends presence to an 8-by-20-foot mail-order greenhouse in Maryland (above). Built of translucent Mylar framed in aluminum, the structure provides state-of-the-art growing conditions for young myrtles and ivy (opposite). Full-grown topiaries stand tall against a salvaged fanlight. Heated with propane, the greenhouse maintains a controlled temperature.**

MANY LOTS HAVE THE yard space for an additional small dwelling if one does not already exist. Constructing an outbuilding from scratch allows homeowners to indulge their wishes—and sometimes their fantasies. There are no rules to be followed, and the level of luxury these spaces achieve becomes a personal decision. Some consider electricity and running water unnecessary amenities in such spaces, creating workshops, fishing huts, conservatories, or potting sheds that are modest, but always

comfortable and efficient. Others find greater enjoyment in building and decorating more elaborate structures where indulgence is key—a secluded guest house for friends and family, a studio where the artistic urge can run free, a children's playhouse where imagination is encouraged. Whatever the choice, building a new structure provides the perfect opportunity to create a haven where reflection and relaxation are inspired.

"When I'm in there I feel like I'm seven years old," says one of the owners of the two-room cabin that they built on their wooded property. Salvaged oversized windows in the cabin's smaller room (it measures 8-by-8) provide unrestricted forest views and ample daylight (top left). In the miniature alcove kitchen of sorts (bottom left), the couple installed as many shelves as possible for storage. Because the cabin lacks running water, meals here are simple affairs. Like a Pullman berth, the cupboard bed epitomizes coziness (opposite). A checked tablecloth became the spread; three cotton dish towels were transformed into cheerful pillowcases. A rescued sidelight used horizontally provides the bunk with a window of its own.

T wo fishing buddies, Craig Bero and Mike Thielke, built an angling hut/fishing cabin by hand on an island in the waters of Little Bear Creek in upstate New York. It has become a nature retreat both for them and for the kids who attend Craig's fishing camp, called The Clearing. They furnished it with rustic antiques and everything necessary for a weekend with rod and reel. A local blacksmith forged the door's cast-iron trout hinges and feathered-salmon fly latch (left). The fishing tackle sign is from a bait shop Craig patronized as a boy. Birch slabs that cover the walls (opposite) once chinked a long cabin near Craig's boyhood home in Wisconsin. Potawatomi artisans berry-painted the speckled trout on the paddle above the doorway. As a boy, Craig cleaned fish on the split-ash table.

T he charms of Victorian style are captured in a diminutive hideaway (above) constructed by a loving grandfather out of recycled materials. A Dutch door and cupboards help little imaginations in the pretend kitchen (top left). To achieve the look of bull's-eye molding on the door and window frames, the owner cut squares of wood, then glued wooden toy wheels in the center of them. A bean bag invites curling up in a corner where painted crates house a juvenile library (bottom left). An abandoned cupboard was recycled to create the beadboard wainscoting. For safety, the owner used Plexiglas instead of glass in most of the windows and auto-detailing tape to create the illusion of panes. No grown-ups are allowed in the snug loft (opposite), which features an air mattress dressed with a vintage chenille pillow and cotton bed linens. A picnic basket serves as a bedside table.

The

PART TWO

Spirit of COUNTRY

ONE OF THE PRIMARY REASONS for the staying power of country style is its refreshing informality. No stiff fabrics, no draperies with tight pleats, no high-gloss finishes. Certainly it's hard to be formal in a room where peeling paint on an object is prized. But living amongst rustic furnishings doesn't mean watching television in a ladderback chair. More and more, country has come to mean real comfort. Sofas and upholstered chairs are slouchy and soft—the kind you can sink into. Fabrics help keep the look easy—mattress ticking, cotton duck, and even on the right piece, super-soft velvet. But comfort can go beyond cushioning. It

Easy Country NEW COMF

can come from cooking in a well-organized space blessed with ample light, soaking in a deep old tub; putting up your feet in a room bathed in light, or simply climbing into a bed that cradles you. ■

ORT

Easy LIVING

A WEEKEND HOME IS supposed to be fuss-free. After all, who wants to worry about cleaning on their time off? A restful spot is what designer Peri Wolfman desired of her newly constructed weekend house on Long Island's shore. To her, restful means simplicity. There is no pattern and only pale colors in the house, except for the worn hues of rustic folk painted pieces. "I don't like spots of color," she explains, "and I have a very hectic life and like my surroundings to be serene." Another reason for the lack of color (and window treatments) was to shift the focus onto the idyllic outdoors. "I wanted the outside to be important," she says, "and to be always looking out." The unpretentious vintage furnishings have clean lines and chipped paint—even new items, such as mirrored medicine cabinets in the master bathroom, were custom made to resemble antique mirrors. Her criteria for upholstered pieces were straightforward: comfortable, simple, and washable. The plump furnishings keep the uncluttered decor from looking too bare bones.

Although the house is newly built, owner Peri Wolfman filled it with plenty of character-imbuing accents such as a vintage table with original paint and the staircase's newel-post, which she discovered at a local antiques show (opposite). White and yellow in all their permutations form an enduring palette for the weekend house. "I wanted a look that was spare but not austere," says Wolfman. In the living room (above), loose slipcovers on fat easy chairs keep the decorating on the informal side. They slip off easily for cleaning.

The bygone touches of the master bathroom (top left) include a cast-iron bathtub and a cutout crescent moon in the door—a humorous reference to old-time outhouses. A half-door in the laundry room (above) opens to reveal a tiny storage space. Wolfman tucked many such spaces into the home to enforce the idea of an old house. A bed crafted from salvaged architectural artifacts and dressed in antique linens presides over the master bedroom (bottom left). An example of creative recycling: Old barn hooks serve as curtain rods on the long windows. A mid-1800 marble-topped French baker's table takes on a new life as a work island in the kitchen (opposite). For a true farmhouse feel, the kitchen's ceiling is deliberately two feet lower than the dining room's.

WHAT MAKES A wonderful living or family room? The answer lies not in filling a space with beautiful fabrics and antiques, but in creating comfort. The homes on these pages have one thing in common—a total lack of pretense. The home-owners were not trying to create showplaces, but spaces where someone could put their feet up on the coffee table, lie down on the sofa, curl up in a big chair, and where children can play. Many are weekend houses, which helps explain the lack of accessories and the slouchy slipcovers. They are places where people want to be outside hiking

Great LIVING AREAS

C reating cozy corners can be a challenge in a space unbroken by walls, but a New Jersey homeowner has done it in her 150-year-old barn-turned-house (opposite). Beside the stairwell, a fat, single-armed chair, draped in a casual slipcover, nestles beside a seven-drawer cherry chest from the Shaker community in New Lebanon, New York. Friendly, informal furnishings also characterize a Maine Victorian. In the living room (above), twin wicker armchairs flank the new beadboard cabinet, which holds a television and VCR.

or lying in the hammock, or inside absorbed in a mystery novel, not worrying about whether the porcelain is dusted. They are owned by people who love their houses and their decorating, but who don't want that to intrude on having fun. "My goal was to create a comfortable, relaxed home in harmony with its surroundings," explains the owner of a North Carolina weekend getaway house. "Its simplicity makes it easy to maintain and a lot safer for the little children who visit us here."

"I wanted this place to feel airy, like a little tree house," says the landscape painter and art teacher who lives in a small apartment, along with her husband and son, in a landmark building in Denver. Though the flat is diminutive, it lives large thanks to sky blue walls in the living room and sun room, white-washed wood floors and large windows left bare to take advantage of the views. The limited number of furnishings are upholstered in pale shades and all are slim in line. "Because the apartment is small, using less made it seem more spacious," she says. The owner inherited the down-filled sofa from her grandmother; her great-grandparents brought the low-slung coffee table home with them after a 1910 trip to Morocco.

F loor-to-ceiling bookshelves bring old-world warmth to a Tudor-style great room (opposite) in a 1914 Connecticut house. The owners divvied up the large room into activity centers to make it more useful. The bookshelves and vintage gaming table turn a corner into a quiet spot for reading and playing games or cards. Set into the side of a cliff overlooking the lush John's River Gorge, a 1930s house in North Carolina possesses both glorious views of the Blue Ridge Mountains and room enough to accommodate visiting children and grandchildren. The wife, an interior designer, shows off her pieces and fabrics in the living/dining area (above) with a cool, classic backdrop of creamy hues and wood floors covered in an eye-calming sisal.

A hand-painted vine and oversized baskets help bring intimacy to a dining bay with a vaulted ceiling (top left). The many-windowed area is paved in tile for easy care. The new pedestal table is crafted of silver maple; the chairs recall the designs of Duncan Phyfe. Though the home is newly built, the architect imbued it with old-house details such as the plaster plaque above the hearth in the living room (left). Doors next to the built-in fireplace disguise the television. Vintage touches enliven another brand-new home (right). Exposed beams lend character to the family room, where loose-fitting, washable cotton slipcovers the amply cushioned seating. One set of aged shutters fills in for a window treatment, another serves as a decorative screen.

EVERYONE LOVES AN old house, but few love an old kitchen. Our way of living—particularly regarding the kitchen—has changed dramatically over the years. The demand is for welcoming, open kitchens that are highly practical and functional, and also work well for several cooks. Ample storage is also an important need, as well as space for dining and entertaining.

There lies the challenge for architects and kitchen designers: how to create a thoroughly modern space with state-of-the art appliances and layout that still has the warmth and character of

Big Family KITCHENS

Vintage ingredients, such as marble-tile countertops, beadboard paneling, and a rebuilt 1913 stove, make a new kitchen (formerly a bedroom) appear timeless in a seaside Victorian (opposite). To delineate the kitchen and dining areas (above) in an 1830s whaler's house, the owner lined the appliances against one wall and used a low pine cupboard as a room divider. The sliver of window above the counter is an upturned transom. The mirror is a feng shui maneuver: its placement "means I never turn my back to the room," the owner explains.

an old house. As the kitchens on these pages illustrate, the secret lies in softening the high-tech necessities with the best of the past. Cabinetry echoes the look of built-in furniture, even down to knobs borrowed from bedroom dressers. Storage is a relaxed mix of open shelving, concealed space, and antique pieces. Texture-giving materials such as wide-plank pine floors, stone (or stone-like synthetic) or tile countertops, and exposed beams made from old wood offer contrast and create interest.

During the 1930s, many kitchens were made with knotty pine cabinetry. In order to retain their home's flavor, the owners of a Depression-era weekend house kept the kitchen (top left) as-is, merely white-washing the cabinets, refinishing the pine floors and topping the cabinets with new countertops of white ceramic tiles. Old-world elements lend charm to a brand-new house as well. Exposed wood beams, a beadboard backsplash, and open shelves combine with soapstone countertops to give character to a newly built home (bottom left). A kitchen addition blends neatly in a 1760s home (opposite). A barn in upstate New York yielded vintage lumber for the flooring, ceiling, beams, and work island. Two shades of stain were used to produce the pattern on the plank floor and cabinet doors. The copper sink receives weekly polishings.

A combination of stunning Federal-style architecture and top-notch design makes an open-plan kitchen one to be envied. Part of a newly constructed townhouse, the kitchen features such classically styled architectural details as a coffered ceiling, custom cabinets, crown moldings, and multipaned windows and transoms (left). Despite the overall size of the space, the work triangle is compact and efficient; the large island (above) holds the range and also separates the cooking and sitting areas. Laminate checkerboard flooring provides continuity and is a practical choice.

THE BEDROOM'S PURPOSE in life is to nurture, restore, and revive. It should be a sanctuary where the responsibilities of life fade away. Create such a place with gentle hues and a bed laden with comfort-yielding elements. On the bed, velvet, silk, or the softest cotton you can find will please the eye and the senses. Such fabrics also look beautiful at the window—especially when full and billowing.

A great view doesn't hurt either. If you have one, keep windows unencumbered. Use light, translucent fabrics, and if hanging drapery, be sure

Bedroom SANCTUARIES

The owners of the Old Drovers Inn in Dover Plains, New York, know much about hospitality. Visitors have stopped at the inn at the foot of the Berkshire Mountains for almost 250 years. Today's owners have concocted gracious bedrooms, such as the Sleigh Room (opposite), distinguished by a velvet-and-satin down-filled duvet on a circa 1930 mahogany bed. A hand-painted weave on the walls makes a spacious bedroom (above) feel more intimate in a new Wisconsin cottage. Filmy curtain panels and a tufted headboard add to the room's allure.

to extend rods well past the sides so that not a stitch of fabric hides the view when the drapes are open. But when selecting window treatments, consider privacy and the need for darkness as well. Room-darkening shades tuck easily behind fabric treatments. Lastly, fill your bedroom with objects you love—a treasured collection, or favorite antique pieces—they will brighten your spirits when you climb into bed at the end of a long day and lift them again when you open your eyes in the morning.

Simplicity in decorating serves two goals in the bedroom of a mountain home (left): It turns attention toward the magnificent scenery and makes life almost carefree for the occupants. The all-white decor is punctuated by a carved reproduction bed and Noguchi paper lamps, which contribute a modern note. Housed in a new wing of a 1790 barn, a master bedroom (above) features aged cypress floors and banks of windows. Octagonal posts and bed hangings accent the cherry bed, a reproduction modeled on an early-19th-century French piece found in Montreal. A painted Vermont blanket chest made in the mid-1800s rests at the foot of the bed.

LIKE KITCHENS, THE most charming bathrooms combine old-fashioned features with modern materials and conveniences. Fortunately, fixture manufacturers are designing a wealth of sinks, vanities, and WCs that recapture the best of period looks and even improve upon them. Custom designs expand the options even further. One popular vanity style is a farm table with two sinks sunk into it. Or an old cabinet can be plumbed and made-over into a vanity.

Creators of tile have brought back many classic looks—oblong subway tile, for instance, or

Indulgent BATHROOMS

T he owner of the house asked her architect to make the master bath (opposite) "as outdoorsy as possible." He complied with a 16-foot ceiling and skylights that allow sunshine to cascade over houseplants that can be lowered by pulley for watering. Distinguished by borders of blue-and-white ceramic tiles, a master bath (above) includes a whirlpool tub and a custom vanity (laden with drawers for storage) with dual sinks and a built-in hamper.

tiny mosaic patterns—and introduced many lovely decorative tiles. As for decorating, improvements in ventilation have enabled designers and homeowners to approach the bathroom more as they would a living space, adding such features as rugs, artwork, and antique chairs, benches or tables, and even displaying collectibles. The bathrooms featured here reflect these trends. There is nothing sterile or cold about them; instead, they are rooms worth lingering in.

entury-old design ideas abound in a new bathroom (top left), including the farmhouse-style table housing two sinks, the honeycomb mosaic floor, and the beadboard on the walls and tub surround. The tub frame of a bathroom (above) owned by a family of Swedish ancestry echoes the built-in look of Swedish beds. Geometrics found in Scandinavian textiles inspired the tile pattern. Walls the color of melted chocolate provide contrast to a white lavatory (bottom left) designed to look like a dressing table. The floor-to-ceiling drapery panel makes the short horizontal window appear longer. The owner of a bathroom (opposite) found a cast-iron tub in an antique store, and had it re-enameled. The 19th-century marble-topped table hails from England.

AT ONE TIME COUNTRY-EVOKING color was limited to either red, white, and blue or the muted hues of Williamsburg. But as country style has evolved, so has our notion of color. New country interiors either boast bold strokes of solid, vibrant color, or are decorated entirely in shades of white or cream with a touch of that favorite of modernists—black.

While subtler in impact than color, texture adds layers of interest to any room. It can be injected through the patterns of age—the crazing of paint on a farm table, the gentle bumps on a stoneware jug—or through more modern touches—a rough sisal rug, a chenille or velvet pillow.

Country patterns, on the other hand, can vary from the classic—gingham or dainty florals—to the unexpected—leather or plaids. Whether used individually as a decorative element, or mixed and matched, creative patterns always bring a room to life. ■

Color, TEXTURE, P

ATTERN

The Power of COLOR

In a living room (page 137) filled with pretty pastel shades , a subtle checkerboard of ceramic tile in earthy tones quietly turns the fireplace (opposite) into a focal point—even when no fire blazes. In contrast to the brilliance of the outdoors, a beach house living room (above) is made up of shades of beige. Art and furniture all belong to the same family of neutrals, while white edging on the upholstered pieces adds subtle contrast.

OF ALL THE WAYS to change a room, color has the most impact. Neutrals are calming and contemporary, pastels add a wink of sweetness, stronger shades fill up a room visually. Furniture should always be a consideration when choosing colors, as some shades enhance the tones in wood, others detract from it. For instance, a green that is too yellow will make the red of cherry appear brassy, but creams, pinks, and beiges will flatter the honey of pine and maple. To set off antiques, walls should be painted all white, or a single shade that complements the wood tones.

Pastel hues make for soothing design. Walls painted an atmospheric blue lend an ethereal quality to a dining room (top left) in a Denver apartment. Knowing that dark pieces would overpower the delicate walls, the homeowner kept floors and furniture light. A bleached wood floor, a pale Swedish-style table, and light late-19th-century Italian lyre-back chairs and bare windows help maintain the room's airy mood. Walls of palest apricot set a serene scene in the cozy sitting room (bottom left) of a two-room Victorian cottage in Sag Harbor, New York. Light-colored floors and creamy furnishings sustain the calm setting. Subtle hints of color come from blue-and-white pillows. Soft colors on the walls wake up an 1840s home in upstate New York (opposite). Refreshing lime-hued walls form the backdrop for furnishings and a rug the colors of sherbet. To make the rug stand out, the chairs and sofa were covered in solids.

n his fashion and home furnishings lines, designer Alexander Julian is known for his flare with color. His own home, which he shares with his wife, Meagan, is equally dazzling. In the dining room (opposite), each leather chair sports a different hue and, with no patterns to distract the eye, the chairs' solid blocks of color add boldness to the space.

"We're not petrified of color," declares restaurant owner Carole Peck of her 1740s Connecticut home. The house, formerly a cider mill, now sports a vibrant palette. Peck's husband, Bernard Jarrier, enlivened the kitchen (above) with salmon-toned walls and then painted cabinetry either a matching salmon shade, chartreuse, or chocolate.

olor—and hard work—brought alive an "almost abandoned property" in Bucks County, Pennsylvania, according to its owners. Since both are in the fashion industry, playing with vivid tones comes naturally to them, which is how the dining room (above) came to have a mango-and-watermelon color scheme with leaf-green trim. One of the owners is French, which explains the Provençal fabric in the old corner cupboard and the French antiques. The brilliant paint scheme makes an eclectic grouping of paintings glow (opposite), and provides a lively backdrop for the antique chairs and a new table modeled after one from the Frenchman's childhood.

Painted HISTORY

Despite the admonitions of mothers everywhere not to draw on the walls, who hasn't had the itch to take brush or pen to that giant canvas? During Colonial times, itinerant painters would travel the country decorating barns and signs and creating paintings and murals. The best known was Rufus Porter, whose naïve, primitive style was copied by Debra Darnall for the sweeping staircase (top left) of an 1848 house in Ohio. One of the great advantages to mural painting is that there is no limit to to the extent that it can reflect personal expression. In the dining room (bottom left) of an 1844 house (now an inn) of 19-century physician A. T. Zevely in Old Salem, North Carolina, a local artist re-created the view that Dr. Zevely would have enjoyed from his upper porch. Although striving for accuracy, the artist still tucked in several references to the present, including the inn's owners' guinea hens and Rosie, a neighbor's Irish setter. To bring pizzazz to the front door of a life-long antiques collector (opposite), a friend, artist Charles Henry James, painted it with rural scenes to remind the owner of the part of Arkansas where she once lived. The moon in the painted pediment was inspired by a grandfather clock in her collection.

LIKE COLORS, PATTERNS can have great impact, but are tricky to mix. The secret to combining patterns is to pick one dominant print, keeping the scale of the room in mind (too small a print and it will be lost in a large room, while an overly large design can overwhelm a small space). Choose complementary patterns that are smaller in scale than the master print, and repeat at least one or two colors in it. To keep a space from becoming too busy, leave blocks of solid color—on the wall or on a large piece of furniture. Take care that the patterns are appropriate for the

Patterns & TEXTURES

surroundings. They should bring out the best in antiques, collectibles, and other pieces.

Texture is the most subtle element of the decorating trio, but when used judiciously it can give a space great richness. To make an impact, texture requires contrast, which can be achieved by mixing various types of fabrics to add punch to furniture, floors, and walls. And of course, patina, which is a subtle way to add texture to a space, is what country furniture has an abundance of.

In the kitchen sitting area of a Connecticut cottage (opposite), jaunty thin-striped club chairs mix with a wide-striped cotton throw rug and a stenciled checkerboard floor. The combination of patterns works because they are all of a different scale but share similar colors. A bold black-and-white checked floor sets an elegant stage for a more formal kitchen seating spot (above). The chair fabric is so intricate and the floor pattern so large that the two blend well.

A homeowner's affection for red comes through in her living room (above), where she paired plaid couches with a striped rug and a polka-dot throw. The mixture works because the plaid is the only small print and the walls are left white for a visual resting place. The owners of another home also co-mingled multiple prints with much success. They designed the living room (left) around the couch and wing chair from their old house. The blue-and-white slipcovered pieces echo the couple's pottery collection and form a base around which red-and-gold-hued fabric revolve. An old quilt inspired the painted pattern of an entryway floor (opposite). The owner used paint left over from painting the trim in other rooms on the first floor. "I wanted to bring in colors from the rooms that open onto the hallway," she explains.

T he play of textures and patterns brings a master-bedroom suite alive (opposite). Wicker chairs painted an unexpected lemon shade set off a nubby dhurrie and a woven club chair and ottoman. For contrast, the cocktail table and floors are smooth and shiny. The exposed beams from the vaulted ceiling introduce yet another pattern. Witty use of prints lends coziness to a two-room 1920s bungalow that serves as play space for the daughters of do-it-yourself decorating doyenne Kitty Bartholomew. With interior designer Stanley Hura, she created a melange of mini-prints in the cottage's study space (top right). But note, there is only one check, one floral, one stripe and one geometric and they are all of the same scale. The main room of the bungalow (bottom right) repeats the blue-and-yellow scheme. "Using a complementary palette from one room to the other visually extends the small space," explains Hura.

Stenciled DRAMA

O nce limited to simple motifs, stenciling has evolved into a complex art form. Skilled stencilers employ multiple tones and patterns to create intricate designs, or they combine freehand painting and stenciling. But stencils are at their best when used to repeat a pattern. At first glance, it seems as if delicate lace adorns the walls of the dining room (below and opposite) of an 1810 farmhouse, but it is actually a damask stencil executed in cream against a taupe wall color. The homeowner—who is also the stencil artist—could have made the effect more subtle by choosing a stencil color that was a few shades lighter or darker than his base color. This pattern was executed with two mylar sheets—the first stencil creates the outline of the pattern, while the overlay provides the finer details.

A few caveats: Measure accurately to ensure that patterns are lined up. Secondly, work with an almost-dry brush and don't wash your brush until you are done stenciling for that day.

COLLECTING HAS ALWAYS BEEN A theme in country decorating. The rules that have defined collecting, however, have relaxed over the past few years. Now lovers of country collectibles have the freedom to set their own parameters and to make the art of collecting a truly personal pursuit. Despite this new freedom, however, the common thread that runs through all country collections is still humbleness. Collectibles are often products of the simplest arts—stenciling, quilting, embroidery, carving, and others—which connect us to another age. American novelist Willa Cather once wrote

New Country COLLECTIB

of "that irregular and intimate quality of things made entirely by the human hand." Perhaps that is why we love handwork so—for its intimacy, and the sense that it offers a window to an earlier time and a glimpse into another person's soul. ■

LES

S ome collectors limit their hunting and gathering to one or two categories and keep them confined in a specific spot. Others joyfully collect a seemingly limitless range of objects and fill every empty niche, any flat surface, with their treasures. In her master bedroom, a highly knowledgeable collector of antique toys displays a winsome group of bisque dolls (top left). Mass produced in the early 1900s, penny toys such as these were eagerly bought and traded by youngsters throughout Great Britain and the U.S. Another chest holds a rare and much-coveted grouping of wooden articulated circus animals (bottom left), clowns and trapeze artists manufactured at the turn of the century in Philadelphia by Albert Schoenhut & Co. In a Los Angeles house, the collectors are less discriminating. When grouping objects they look for one thing—color. Folksy painted shelves in their kitchen (opposite) display such eclectic ceramics as South American jitney buses, Mexican-motif 1940s dinner plates made by Edwin Knowles China, and a Quimper pitcher and plate.

C ollectors get bitten by the bug in different ways. Twenty years ago, a Connecticut couple first spied a pair of blue-and-white Canton china water jugs in a Rhode Island antiques shop. Many pieces later, they show off their trove in a circa 1840 Irish pine cupboard (top left). Sometimes, collectors run out of room. An aficionado of green glass is almost at such a point. In her kitchen, green-glass objects (known as jadeite) ranging from egg cups to mixing bowls almost overwhelm an old cupboard (bottom left). Plenty of ingenuity and a pure love of collecting can readily be seen in a Midwestern collector's 1844 cottage. The retired antiques dealer fashioned the cocktail table in his living room (opposite) by cradling an 1860s dough bowl in the legs of an inverted twig table. He crafted the twin lamps that flank the 1850 daybed from Civil War shell casings. Shelves display an extensive collection of Galena and Rockingham-glaze pottery. The giant key and spectacles were tradesmen's signs.

Can farmhouse furnishings reside happily in the most urban environment of all? In a New York City apartment, the answer is yes. The tiny flat is home to such varied pieces as a circa 1865 sponge-painted chest and a set of wooden carved puppets from the 1920s. The collector marries different objects by stacking pieces on top of each other—literally—and by keeping the setting pristine. "I prefer interiors with white walls, mirrors, and hardwood floors for displaying folk art," he says. The bold graphic quality of his art intensifies against a cool backdrop. Old game boards (above) look like pop art when hung on walls. An antique step stool sits below them.

A devoted gardener, collector, and self-described lover of rust and old paint combines his passions in an 800-square-foot stone home, a former toll house. In the tiny entry (above), carefully pruned topiaries of myrtle, rosemary, and lavender stand beside vintage garden sprinklers. More sprinklers parade up the stairs (left). Above them hang gilt-framed mirrors. Several of the frames were empty when the owner found them; he liked the way they looked so much he hung them as they were. Like the trumpet section of an orchestra, a group of old American and English watering cans stand at the ready on a weathered, painted shelf (opposite).

American FIESTA

With its streamlined shape, billiard-ball finish, and enticing colors, once humble Fiestaware has become a valuable collectible. In 1936, the Homer Laughlin China Co. first introduced the casual dinnerware, designed by pottery designer Fredrick H. Rhead. An exhibit at the 1939 New York World's Fair popularized what was then very modern-looking dishware. To a collector of Fiestaware, color is one of the best indicators of price. Because certain colors were made only during specific periods, the color of a piece can reveal its age. Originally, Fiestaware was sold in five colors: ivory, yellow, cobalt blue, light green, and orange red. In 1943 the production of red—which contained uranium oxide in its glaze—was halted at the request of the Atomic Energy Commission. Production of the entire line stopped in 1969, but the original patterns (in slightly different hues) were re-introduced in 1994 and are available today.

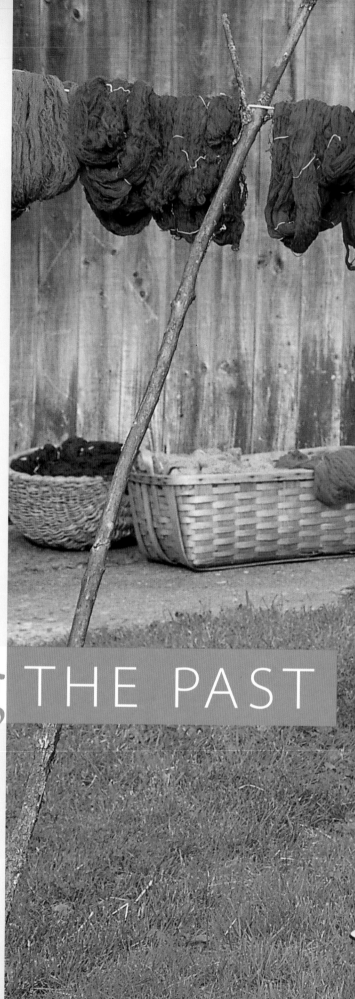

WHILE MOST OF US HEAD TO AN office to labor in front of a computer, there are still many people whose "work" is creating and preserving the past. For such people, there is no line between home and work, and they approach both with a sense of mission, for they see themselves as a needed link to an almost forgotten past. Dreamers they may be, but their goal is clear—they seek to hold onto that which is fast disappearing, before the old ways and the objects that were created using them are gone forever.

Some of these folks seek to recreate old arts, such as weaving, pottery, and carpentry, with techniques and materials that

Re-creating THE PAST

may have been popular a century ago. Others follow the *spirit* of earlier times and act as preservationists. All celebrate the beauty of the past to make a more beautiful present and future. ▪

In her Vermont home, weaver Kate Smith works with antique looms, natural dyes, and authentic techniques to recreate 18th- and 19th-century textiles. She spins and dyes the yarn herself, using flowers and herbs from her garden. Inspiration for her designs comes from museums, tag sale fabric remnants, and photographs from books and magazines.

An old cupboard serves as display space for Kate Smith's textile samples (left). Her handwoven textiles bring color and old-fashioned warmth to a bedroom (opposite). A striped fabric known as linsey-woolsey serves as a curtain, while her own carpeting covers the floor. An indigo-banded wool throw covers a quilt with a madder-dyed worsted-wool top and an indigo-dyed worsted-wool backing. A checked indigo-dyed wool blanket covers the bed.

DON CARPENTIER built Eastfield Village, in upstate New York, as a workshop for students wishing to learn the art of restoration. The village, dotted with more than twenty turn-of-the-century buildings, was painstakingly rebuilt using traditional building techniques, and is dedicated to preserving a simpler way of life.

A mong the structures in Eastfield's 14-acre site is the Yellow Tavern (above), a popular gathering place for students at Eastfield, who cook on the open hearth and experience lodging without electricity or running water. The village's Cady Brown general store dates to 1811. Its shelves (opposite) are no longer filled with goods, however. They hold reproduction 19th-century polychrome pearlware made by Carpentier's wife, Denise.

A Horse FARM

In the old days, barns in cold areas were often attached to the house so that a farmer would not have to go outside in the winter to care for the animals. These owners recreated that look with their own house and three-story barn (above). The front door (opposite) offers a view to the north of the Adirondack Mountains. Old glass panes in the transom and sidelights ripple the light. In the entry, pine floorboards, original to the house, measure more than a foot in width. Scrollwork on the stair was removed and stripped of layers of paint before being reattached.

WITH ITS MAJESTIC ANIMALS and long stretches of green pastures, a horse farm is perhaps the most lovely of all working homes. A farm in Saratoga Springs, New York, is just such a place. Though it is a place of serious horse-raising, beauty abounds. The attractiveness of the spot is only enhanced by the 1757 house and the collection of barns and stables surrounding it. To all appearances, it would seem that these structures had been on this spot overlooking the Adirondacks forever. But in reality, the house and many of the barns are all salvaged structures from around New England. Each had been slated for demolition and was bought, restored, and rebuilt by Vermont-based Weather Hill Restoration Co. Only the actual horse barn—a reproduction—is new.

The buildings are all rich in architectural details. The house's front door, for example, features finely carved millwork, and cupolas adorn every barn on the farm.

The farmhouse kitchen combines a 19th-century mood with modern efficiency (top left). Hand-hewn beams contrast nicely with granite countertops and a gleaming copper hood. The wainscoting and cabinetry were crafted in Weather Hill Restoration's shop. Two sets of reproduction French doors define the dining area (bottom left) and keep it flooded with light. As was often the case in the old days, a rug serves as a tablecloth. The keeping room (opposite), opening directly into the dining area and the kitchen, is a cozy place. The millwork around the fireplace was stripped of paint, then waxed and buffed. Although many of the pieces in the room are reproductions, the grain-painted table showcasing the homeowners' photographs is 200 years old.

n the 1700s and 1800s, such a public room as a front parlor was inevitably lavished with as much intricate millwork as a family could afford (private spaces such as bedrooms, however, were left plain). This front parlor is a perfect example. Such sought-after architectural assets as dentil moldings, deep windows, paneled wainscoting, and the original mantel, give it elegance.

The owners deliberately kept the decorating formal but not fancy, to allow the architecture to stand out. The walls are a gentle colonial gray, for instance. A trio of old horse portrait lithographs lines the wall. Reproduction pewter sconces flank the fireplace and frame a collection of various racing trophies won by the couple's thoroughbred horses.

WHAT MAKES COUNTRY GATHERINGS so delightful? They have a natural informality that puts guests and hosts at ease, with no formal flower arrangements or courtly settings to intimidate. But, country entertaining doesn't preclude grace and glamour. Large gatherings and intimate dinners alike benefit from a dose of drama. Abundant candlelight—and unusual candleholders—instantly conveys a festive air. Bunches of fresh flowers picked from the garden add color and scent to any gathering.

Planning an event is an excuse to let the imagination go and have fun. Decide whether the event calls for thirty guests to mingle poolside for an afternoon luncheon, or for six friends to savor the luxury of a formal indoor dinner. The cardinal rules still apply: Keep things simple; use tableware and furnishings already on hand in creative new ways; and incorporate the natural world into both the menu and the decor. ■

Home ENTERTAIN

When the weather is balmy and the mosquitoes are at bay, nothing beats outdoor dining. A farmyard (opposite) becomes the setting for an anniversary party, transformed by an awning. Vintage tables hold food and tableware; champagne stays cold in an old wheelbarrow. Against the cornfield, a bank of tables is dressed in lengths of checked fabric. Ironstone pitchers overflow with hydrangea and hold the tablecloth in place. Masses of bougainvillea turn a pergola into a shady retreat for al fresco dining in a California garden (above). Interplanted to form a single canopy, the bougainvillea blooms from March to November. The 10-foot-long table was designed by the owner, who used Portuguese tiles and an iron base. The table decorations are appropriately relaxed: A large bunch of just-picked goldenrod stands in a florist's bucket, while lemons are placed about the table as bright props.

For two busy professional chefs, the kitchen is the only place to entertain. When they built a Georgia farmhouse a few years ago, they ensured that their kitchen was equipped to handle serious cooking and hospitality. "We can feed a large group in a snap," says one of the owners. A freestanding fireplace separates the kitchen and dining area from the living room (left). The hefty pine table can easily seat 14; its rough patina is offset by steel chairs dressed in tie-on seat covers. The kitchen (above) can be spiffed up in a flash—thanks to concrete floors and stainless steel counters. Purple onion blooms (from the couple's garden) punctuate a portable worktable that doubles as a breakfast bar.

A small dinner gathering has the mood of outdoor dining thanks to ivy-covered walls (above). When the owners rebuilt an old barn, the contractor added an 18-inch trench around the perimeter of the living area so that ivy could be trained to climb up the walls. The juxtaposition of the old with the new lends character to another former barn. A butcher's chopping block is now the dining table, its surface civilized with white paint, shoe polish, and beeswax (right). Old office chairs lacquered red make comfortable dining chairs. Eucalyptus leaves, bittersweet, and other botanicals provide a lush backdrop for a Thanksgiving feast (opposite). Galax-leaf "place cards" display the guests' names inscribed in gold ink.

INDEX

PHOTOGRAPHY CREDITS

1 Jessie Walker

2 Jessie Walker

4–5 Steven Randazzo

6–7 Keith Scott Morton

8 William Steele

10 (top) Alan Weintraub

10 (middle) Keith Scott Morton

10 (bottom) Keith Scott Morton

12–13 Keith Scott Morton

14 Keith Scott Morton

15 (both) Keith Scott Morton

16–17 (both) Keith Scott Morton

18 (both) Keith Scott Morton

19 (all) Keith Scott Morton

20–21 (both) Steven Mays

22 Jessie Walker

23 (both) Jessie Walker

24 (all) Keith Scott Morton

25 Keith Scott Morton

26 Jessie Walker

27 (both) Jessie Walker

28 Keith Scott Morton

29 Keith Scott Morton

30–31 (both) Jessie Walker

32 (all) Keith Scott Morton

33 Keith Scott Morton

34–35 (both) Alan Weintraub

36 Mark Lohman

37 Mark Lohman

38 (all) Mark Lohman

39 Mark Lohman

40 (both) Jessie Walker

41 Jessie Walker

42 Keith Scott Morton

43 (both) Keith Scott Morton

44 Lisl Dennis

45 (all) Lisl Dennis

46 Jeremy Samuelson

47 Keith Scott Morton

48–49 Keith Scott Morton

50 Keith Scott Morton

51 Keith Scott Morton

52–53 (both) Keith Scott Morton

54 (both) Keith Scott Morton

55 Keith Scott Morton

56 (both) Keith Scott Morton

57 Keith Scott Morton

58 Keith Scott Morton

59 Keith Scott Morton

60–61 Keith Scott Morton

62 (both) Keith Scott Morton

63 Keith Scott Morton

64 Steven Mays

65 Steven Mays

66 Steven Mays

67 Steven Mays

68–69 Keith Scott Morton

70 Keith Scott Morton

71 Keith Scott Morton

72–73 Keith Scott Morton

74 Keith Scott Morton

75 (both) Keith Scott Morton

76–77 (both) Keith Scott Morton

78–79 (all) Keith Scott Morton

80 Tony Giammarino

81 Tony Giammarino

82 Tony Giammarino

83 (both) Tony Giammarino

84–85 (both) Keith Scott Morton

86 Steven Mays

87 Steven Mays

88 Keith Scott Morton

89 Keith Scott Morton

90–91 (all) Keith Scott Morton

92–93 Keith Scott Morton

94 Keith Scott Morton

95 (both) Keith Scott Morton

96 Keith Scott Morton

97 (both) Keith Scott Morton

98 Keith Scott Morton

99 Keith Scott Morton

100 (both) Kari Haavisto

101 Kari Haavisto

102 Keith Scott Morton

103 Keith Scott Morton

104 (all) Jessie Walker

105 Jessie Walker

106 (top) Keith Scott Morton

106 (middle) Keith Scott Morton

106 (bottom) Kari Haavisto

108–109 Keith Scott Morton

110 Keith Scott Morton

111 Keith Scott Morton

112 (all) Keith Scott Morton

113 Keith Scott Morton

114 Keith Scott Morton

115 Keith Scott Morton

116–117 Keith Scott Morton

118 Steven Mays

119 Keith Scott Morton

120–121 (all) Keith Scott Morton

122 Keith Scott Morton

123 William Steele

124 (both) Keith Scott Morton

125 Keith Scott Morton

126 Keith Scott Morton

127 Keith Scott Morton

128 Steven Randazzo

129 Keith Scott Morton

130 Keith Scott Morton

131 Keith Scott Morton

132 Keith Scott Morton

133 Jessie Walker

134 (top left) Keith Scott Morton

134 (top right) Keith Scott Morton

134 (bottom) Jessie Walker

135 Keith Scott Morton

136–137 Keith Scott Morton

138 Keith Scott Morton

139 Keith Scott Morton

140 (both) William Steele

141 Steven Randazzo

142 Keith Scott Morton

143 Keith Scott Morton

144–145 (both) Keith Scott Morton

146 (top) Jessie Walker

146 (bottom) Keith Scott Morton

147 Jessie Walker

148 Keith Scott Morton

149 Keith Scott Morton

150 (both) Keith Scott Morton

151 Keith Scott Morton

152 Kari Haavisto

153 (both) Grey Crawford

154 Keith Scott Morton

155 Keith Scott Morton

156–157 Jeremy Samuelson

158 (both) Pizzi/Thompson

159 Mark Lohman

160 (both) Keith Scott Morton

161 Jessie Walker

162–163 (both) Keith Scott Morton

164 (both) Keith Scott Morton

165 Keith Scott Morton

166 Kari Haavisto

167 Polly Wreford of Robert Harding, Inc.

168–169 Keith Scott Morton

170 Keith Scott Morton

171 Keith Scott Morton

172 Keith Scott Morton

173 Keith Scott Morton

174 Keith Scott Morton

175 Keith Scott Morton

176 (both) Keith Scott Morton

177 Keith Scott Morton

178–179 Keith Scott Morton

180–181 Charles Gold

182 Charles Gold

183 Mark Lohman

184–185 (both) Keith Scott Morton

186 (both) Keith Scott Morton

187 Keith Scott Morton

192 Jessie Walker